What Matters

We are born. We die.
What happens in between is up to us.

Written By Phil Rainwater
Arranged by Moira Callaghan

For the Benefit of the Pancreatic Cancer Action Network

For my three sons Colt, James, and Tim,
and for my loving wife Bai.

Without you, this book would not be.

These quotes are my Legacy. I call them "What Matters."
And you have mattered most to me.

And to Moira,
For her big, sweet heart, her boundless endurance, and her all-around wonderfulness.

Printed in Hong Kong.
First Printing, 2018
ISBN 978-0-69-218565-0

Benchmark Communications, Inc.
21545 Ridgetop Circle
Sterling, VA 20166

Visit: whatmattersbooks.com

Prologue

I have three sons. For them, as a legacy, I wrote a series of original, short quotes, attached to my Last Will and Testament. I called these quotes, "What Matters."

This book is a compilation from those quotes. Are the quotes 100% original? I think so, but I am sure outside sources have unconsciously influenced my ideas and text.

What Matters

We all are in the same predicament: our life is finite, our future opaque.

And when finality does come, is there one more thing we wish we would have done, or done differently? Will there be one more thing we wish we would have said?

Good or bad, seemingly fair or not—our life's outcome is up to us. It may not seem so, but it is so. Such is the glory of our lives, and such is the burden of our lives . . . which we create, and recreate, moment by moment.

We make choices. Our life happens. *What Matters* is about those choices.

Charity Partner: The Pancreatic Cancer Action Network

Cancer kills. And pancreatic kills, mercilessly. If discovered, there is a 91% probability of dying within 5 years. But there is hope, and effort, to improve these grim odds, and it is the Pancreatic Cancer Action Network ("PanCAN"), and its Purple Stride and Purple Light Events.

The Pancreatic Cancer Action Network honors loved ones who are fighting pancreatic cancer, and honors those who have lost the battle.

It is a global organization that seeks to build awareness for Pancreatic Cancer, to promote funding for research, and to support stricken patients.

In 2018, pancreatic cancer is the 3rd leading cause of cancer deaths. It has the highest mortality rate of all leading cancers.

Sharing of Sales Proceeds: 60% to Our Causes . . .

Fifty percent (50%) of the net proceeds from the sale of this book will be donated to the Pancreatic Cancer Action Network.

Ten percent (10%) of the net sale proceeds will be donated jointly to the PTA of Buzz Aldrin Elementary School, Reston, VA and to the Greater Reston Arts Center, VA.

That which we choose
not to try . . .

will be forever
that which we do not know.

Sophia Tarazi, age 12, Nysmith School for the Gifted, Herndon, VA—
ink and color pencil on paper.

Chance and circumstance determine
our destiny,

but we determine the likelihood
of our chance and circumstance.

Saloni Dalal, age 11—
acrylic on canvas.

If you are not winning,

change how you approach winning.

Amara Brown, Buzz Aldrin Elementary, Reston, VA—
tempera on paper.

Find time for

the children in your life . . .

and all other time

will find its place.

Dominique Kalunga, age 12, Buzz Aldrin Elementary, Reston, VA—
tempera on paper.

In order to make a difference,

you may need to be different.

Joshua Gregory, age 10, Buzz Aldrin Elementary, Reston, VA—
cut paper.

Life is the ultimate IQ test,

and the score changes daily.

Conner Sulfstede, age 12, Langston Hughes Middle School, Reston, VA—
marker and pencil on paper.

Do not make memories

that you must run from.

Maximus Nasta, age 12, Armstrong Elementary, Reston, VA—
pen, marker, and crayon on paper.

To be liked by others,
is it necessary

to be the same as others?

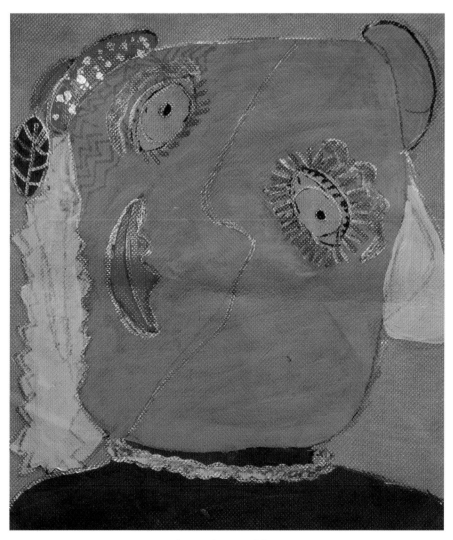

Amanda, age 10—
fabric paint on canvas.

Many years from now,

maybe I will not matter . . .

except how I mattered

to my children.

Campbell Krider, Kindergarten, Buzz Aldrin Elementary, Reston, VA—
crayon on paper.

The ability
to articulate what you want,
and achieving what you want . . .

bear a high correlation.

Brandt Michael Rogers, age 12, Cooper Middle School, McLean, VA—
acrylic on paper.

Extra attention to details . . .
separates

exceptional from average.

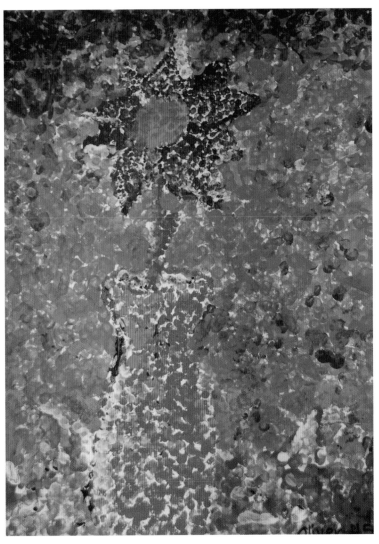

Oliver, age 11, Sunrise Valley Elementary, Reston, VA—
tempera on paper.

Time with your children
is like no other
time in your life.

Make it count.

Francesca, age 7, Lake Anne Elementary, Reston, VA—
marker on paper.

To be extraordinary,

live extraordinarily.

Bryn Yenesel, age 11, Sunrise Valley Elementary, Reston, VA—
acrylic on paper.

You can never make your parents too proud,

but you sure can try.

Gabrielle McClellan, age 12, Sunrise Valley Elementary, Reston, VA—
marker and watercolor on paper.

Awareness of dying . . .
greatly increases

the awareness of living.

MacKenzie Krider, Reston, VA—
pen and color pencil on paper.

If we are really smart . . .

do we think that we are smart,

or do we think we are not so smart?

Darya Regaswamy, age 8—
tempera paint and marker on paper.

Effort:
When you give your best, it shows.

When you don't give your best, it also shows.

Emily Diaz, age 9, Lake Anne Elementary, Reston, VA—
cut paper.

All knowledge leads to
less knowledge.

The more we know, the more
we realize
what we don't know.

Hannah Wilson-Black, age 13, Langston Hughes Middle, Reston, VA—
color pencil on paper.

It takes an uncommon mind
to see

what is common among minds.

Ella Rae, age 9 —
marker on paper.

If you do not fit in,

do not force the fit.

Casey Henson, age 10, Buzz Aldrin Elementary, Reston, VA—
oil pastel on paper.

One of the certainties in life
is that we will experience
uncertainty,

and probably lots of it.

Luke Rowe, age 9, Buzz Aldrin Elementary, Reston, VA—
tempera on paper.

Because you live,
the world may or may not be
a better place,

but that's up to you.

Catherine, Terraset Elementary, Reston, VA —
crayon and water color on paper.

Time and opportunity . . .
stand still for no one.

and neither are recoverable.

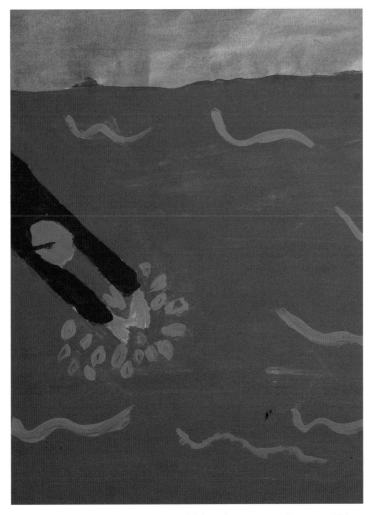

Sara Sorenson, age 12, Buzz Aldrin Elementary, Reston, VA—
tempera on paper.

Live boldly . . .

but survive.

Olivia Rose —
tempera paint on paper.

Knowledge is about
how to do something.

Wisdom is about
why to do something.

Kaliyana Haering, age 11, Sunrise Valley Elementary, Reston, VA—
tempera on paper.

People must know
not only what you stand against,
they must know what you stand for.

There is a big difference.

Luke, age 9, Sunrise Valley Elementary, Reston, VA—
tempera on paper.

We cannot suffer
with all in the world who suffer,
but we can choose

never to cause suffering.

James Chadwick, age 6, Sunrise Valley Elementary, Reston, VA—
water color on paper.

My heart says I will build a hundred
ships, and I will sail a hundred seas.
My mind says that is impossible.

Do I build a hundred ships, or do I
wonder, for all my life, if I should have
built a hundred ships?

Elissa, age 10 —
oil pastel on paper.

When your health

talks to you, listen.

Shylah Swope, age 7—
acrylic paint on canvas.

Adventures teach us

what we can learn

no other way.

Callahan, Buzz Aldrin Elementary, Reston, VA—
tempera on paper.

What we choose not to do,

as much as what we choose to do,
defines us.

Nathan Naveen, age 7, Sunrise Valley Elementary, Reston, VA—
marker, crayon and water color on paper.

Don't save your
best effort for last.

It should be your only effort.

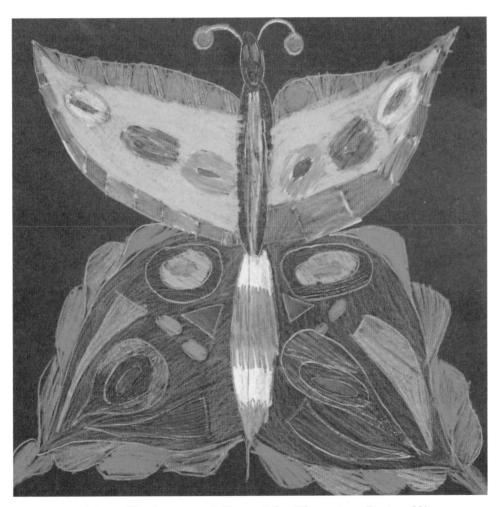

Dominique Giordano, age 9, Forest Edge Elementary, Reston, VA—
color pencil on paper.

To be remembered,
do something well,

and do it often.

Christopher Zhong, age 10, Sunrise Valley Elementary, Reston, VA—
marker, color pencil, and oil pastel on paper.

Inspiration
can lead a team to victories

that intimidation cannot.

Brian Boyce, age 10, Lake Anne Elementary, Reston, VA—
tempera on paper.

In a choice
between right and wrong,

is there a choice?

Katie Raust, age 10, Buzz Aldrin Elementary, Reston, VA—
water color on paper.

Angry words inflict
wounds that never heal,
scars that never vanish,
and pain that never ceases.

Lilly Khalkho—
oil pastel on paper.

Force or finesse:

Do we push our way in
or ease our way in?

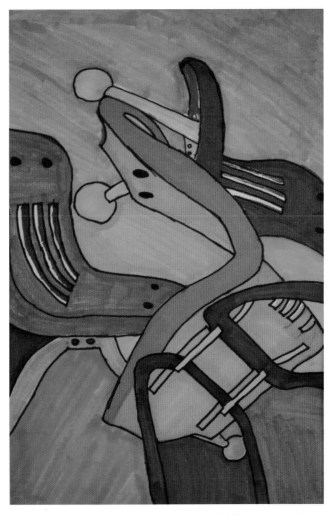

Isabelle Saillard, age 12, Langston Hughes Middle School, Reston, VA—
marker on paper.

Do not expect the people
for whom you do not have time . . .

to ever have time for you.

Caroline Morehouse, age 10, Great Falls Elementary, Great Falls, VA—
acrylic on canvas.

Multi-tasking: a recipe

for multi-mediocrity.

Max Norcross, age 11, Buzz Aldrin Elementary, Reston, VA—
cut paper.

No matter how great your talents,

always be a teammate.

Maddie, age 10, Buzz Aldrin Elementary, Reston, VA—
tempera on paper.

About change:
adapt or perish.

Sitting on the sidelines
is not an option.

Elizabeth, age 8—
oil pastel on paper.

Adventures are for
the adventurous.

All others can hear their tales,
or read their books.

Nicholas Garbing, age 7, Buzz Aldrin Elementary, Reston, VA—
tempera on paper.

Is it better to be smart or lucky?

It depends on how smart you are . . .

when you are lucky.

Catherine Gillespie, age 10, Great Falls Elementary, Great Falls, VA—
acrylic on paper.

A prayer is not an event,

it is an experience.

Haley, age 10, Crossfield Elementary, Herndon, VA—
acrylic on canvas.

A child's love is pure.

Return it purely.

Chloe, Buzz Aldrin Elementary, Reston, VA—
marker and color pencil on paper.

Mediocrity:
the path of least resistance,
the road of least effort,

and the journey of least meaning.

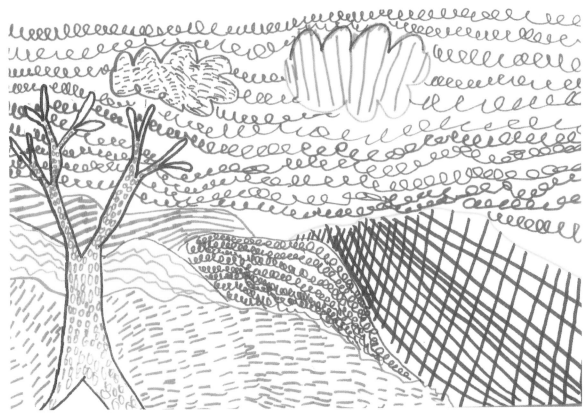

David Raw, age 10, Oak Hill Elementary, Herndon, VA—
marker on paper.

If I could see tomorrow,

what would I change today?

Jenna Mangis —
color pencil on paper.

To really live,

understand death.

Samantha Gloe, age 13, Langston Hughes Middle School, Reston, VA—
pen and pencil on paper.

Great marriages
are born of love,

then sustained by trust.

Ella Hovermale, age 8, Terraset Elementary, Reston, VA—
marker on paper.

There is nothing about me
that cannot be made better tomorrow.

Katie Semanchik, age 7, Armstrong Elementary, Reston, VA—
oil pastel on paper.

Epilogue One: The Pancreatic Cancer Action Network

Pancreatic cancer recently surpassed breast cancer as the 3rd leading cause of cancer-related deaths. It is projected to become the 2nd leading cause of cancer-related deaths by 2020.

Because there are currently no early detection tools or curative treatments, just 9% of those diagnosed will survive more than 5 years. It is the only major cancer with a 5-year relative survival rate in the single digits, a survival rate that has not changed in 4 decades! In 2018, an estimated 55,400 Americans will be diagnosed with pancreatic cancer and 44,300 will die from the disease. This is not acceptable!

But there is HOPE! It is called The Pancreatic Cancer Action Network (PanCAN). PanCAN is a national organization creating hope in a comprehensive way through research, patient support, community outreach, and advocacy for a cure. PanCAN's mission is to double the survival rate by 2020.

PanCAN's signature fundraiser is Purple Stride. Every year in communities across the country, thousands of people participate in Purple Stride. These events range in size from brief walks to timed-runs, but they all share one goal: to end pancreatic cancer and honor those who are in their battle, those that have lost their battle, and more importantly, give hope to those that that will face the battle. It is a journey toward hope that is filled with inspiration. To learn more about PanCAN, go to www.pancan.org.

As part of PanCAN's passionate volunteer community, I cannot express in words my sincere gratitude for PanCAN being selected as a recipient of part of the proceeds from the sale of this unique and outstanding book, *What Matters*. The quotes are wonderful and the illustrations are fascinating.

What Matters speaks to finding purpose and meaning in our lives, amidst seemingly endless choices and their consequences. Thank you for choosing to help us to change the story of pancreatic cancer by purchasing this book. And please continue to follow us and support us.

Sincerely,

Nancy Mader

Atlanta Volunteer Advocacy Chair
Pancreatic Cancer Action Network

Epilogue Two: Compiled in 2014; Published in 2018.

Moira and I assembled this book in 2014.

Our ability to publish was delayed, but we never gave up on the project.

The power and the glory of this book is the art of the these children.

Four years later, these images are still wonderful, timeless, and striking.

Thank you.

Phil Rainwater

Artists

Thanks and Gratitude

We wish to thank all of the artists and their parents and guardians for the support and encouragement for this book.

We are honored to have their visions and creativity, illustrating *What Matters* with innocence, imagination, inspiration, and pure hearts. Their art gave life to this book, giving wings to the words and allowing the meanings to soar beyond the pages.

And we wish to extend special, heartfelt thanks to:

Kyle Anderson, Art Teacher, GRACE Arts Summer Camp, Reston, VA.

Cheri Danaher, Arts Education Director, Reston Community Center, Reston, VA.

Amanda Davis, Art Teacher, Buzz Aldrin Elementary, Reston, VA.

Kim Gilbreath, PTA President, Buzz Aldrin Elementary, Reston, VA.

Karen Graham , Owner, Children's Art Studio of Great Falls, Great Falls, VA.

Lauren Hensen, Art Teacher, GRACE Arts Summer Camp, Reston, VA.

Kris Johnson, Art Teacher, Lake Anne Elementary, Reston, VA.

Jeanne Loveland, Director, Greater Reston Arts Center (GRACE), Reston, VA.

Stephanie Steinmetz, Art Teacher, Buzz Aldrin Elementary, Reston, VA.

Mary Beth Swicord, Owner, First Marks Art Studio, Reston, VA.

Heather Warstler, Art Teacher, Sunrise Valley Elementary, Reston, VA.

Shane Wolfe, Principal, Buzz Aldrin Elementary, Reston, VA.